Nap and Nod

12 ADORABLE BABY QUILTS

MYRA HARDER

Martingale
Create with Confidence

DEDICATION

- To Samson and Robyn, the two little ones who came into my life and changed my world. I didn't know two small babies could teach me the biggest lessons I needed to learn. You will always be my pride and my joy.
- And to Mark, who has been by my side, dragging me through every adventure. Without you, I would be bored.

Nap and Nod:

12 Adorable Baby Quilts

© 2014 by Myra Harder

Martingale®

19021 120th Ave. NE, Ste. 102

Bothell, WA 98011-9511 USA

ShopMartingale.com

Printed in China

19 18 17 16 15 14   8 7 6 5 4 3 2 1

Library of Congress Cataloging-in-Publication Data is available upon request.

ISBN: 978-1-60468-377-6

MISSION STATEMENT

Dedicated to providing quality products and service to inspire creativity.

CREDITS

PRESIDENT AND CEO: Tom Wierzbicki

EDITOR IN CHIEF: Mary V. Green

DESIGN DIRECTOR: Paula Schlosser

MANAGING EDITOR: Karen Costello Soltys

ACQUISITIONS EDITOR: Karen M. Burns

TECHNICAL EDITOR: Nancy Mahoney

COPY EDITOR: Sheila Chapman Ryan

PRODUCTION MANAGER: Regina Girard

COVER AND INTERIOR DESIGNER: Adrienne Smitke

PHOTOGRAPHER: Brent Kane

ILLUSTRATOR: Anne Moscicki

Contents

INTRODUCTION 5

TWO WAYS TO APPLIQUÉ 7

EMBELLISHING YOUR QUILT 9

FINISHING YOUR QUILT 13

♣ PROJECTS

Twinkle, Twinkle 17

Playpen 23

Sandbox 27

Gummy Bears 33

Picking Pansies 37

Birthday Bash 41

Swimming Lessons 45

Gumdrops 53

Peas in a Pod 59

Hunter's Star 65

Jack's Boxes 71

Gift-Wrapped 75

ACKNOWLEDGMENTS 79

ABOUT THE AUTHOR 80

Introduction

Finding out you're going to have a baby is one of the best things that many of us could wish to hear, and August 19, 1999, was a day I'll always remember. Two things happened that day. First, I got a phone call at 7:00 p.m. from Martingale, telling me that they were excited about a book proposal I had submitted, and they were going to publish my first book, Down in the Valley (2001), that I coauthored with Cori Derksen. Later that same night, I found out that I was pregnant. I found out I was going to be an author and a mom on the same night. I was excited, I was nervous, and I didn't know which adventure was going to scare me more.

Martingale gave my coauthor and me an eight-month time frame to finish the quilts and write the book, which was going to be published in April. The doctor gave me the same news—I was due to give birth sometime in the month of April! As it turns out, we shipped off our manuscript on April 1, and my son arrived just 16 days later.

You might wonder when I had time to get my nursery ready, and the truth is I really didn't. In between sewing and writing, I gathered together a crib and baby clothes. I bought a few things, borrowed other items from friends, and learned that this was only the beginning of everything a child would need. And like many expectant mothers, I wanted to make the perfect baby quilt.

I thought this would be the easiest part of creating my nursery. What I quickly discovered was that I could not come up with a single idea for a quilt! I would plan, replan, overthink, change color palettes, and start over from scratch. I don't know if it was the pressure of getting it right or the raging hormones, but I couldn't focus enough to design a single baby quilt! Thanks to the grace of others, however, my son had a small collection of beautiful quilts to keep him warm.

In the spring of 2002, history repeated itself. I signed contracts for two books with Martingale, and discovered I was pregnant the same week! Again, it turned out that I could design every type of project except for a baby quilt. And again it was from the kindness of others that my little girl was wrapped in perfect baby quilts.

It's been a decade since I had my last baby, and I can finally think of all the great quilts I would like to have made. This book is a collection of some of these ideas. You'll find that some projects have traditional roots, while others have a distinctly more modern feel. I hope you'll find the quilts fast and fun to make, and that you'll enjoy creating a quilt for a very special little someone. And maybe you'll want to make a few to keep on hand, because you never know when you'll meet a pregnant quilter who desperately needs a baby quilt.

~Myra

Two Ways to Appliqué

When I was creating the quilts for this book, I knew some would need a touch of appliqué. I'm familiar with the traditional needle-turn appliqué method, and I always believed it was the "proper" way to appliqué. However, when I designed the "Gummy Bears" quilt on page 33, I thought, "Wouldn't it be fun if the bears were soft?" This little idea began my new love affair with plush fabrics—and raw-edge appliqué.

APPLIQUÉ THE PLUSH WAY

I think many of us adore the supersoft feel of plush fabrics, but we find them difficult to use. These fabrics don't act the same way cotton does. Plush fabrics are stretchy and thick, so using them in traditional piecing may cause you to cuss. However, I've found that they're great when paired with traditional cotton fabrics—the cotton adds the stability that the plush needs. In some of the baby quilts in this book, I use pieces of appliquéd plush; it's fast and easy to use, but most of all, it adds a wonderful softness for snuggling Baby.

Follow these steps when appliquéing with plush fabric:

1. Trace the appliqué shape onto a piece of thin cardboard. Cut out your appliqué shape on the drawn line. Do not add a seam allowance. Note that the patterns for plush appliqué are shown as the reverse of the finished block.

2. Use a ballpoint pen or an ultra-thin Sharpie marker to trace the appliqué shape on the wrong side of the plush fabric.

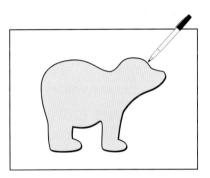

3. Using a good pair of scissors, cut out the plush-fabric shape on the drawn line. Do not add a seam allowance. **Warning:** This is not a good day to wear black, because when you cut plush fabric, it will create fuzz! This is the worst part of working with the fabric, but once you're through this step, everything else is easy. Once the fabric is cut, some of the edges may give you some fuzz, but after you've pulled the fuzz from the edges, it will never fuzz again. Just keep your vacuum handy and you'll be fine.

4. Position the appliqué shape on the quilt, and secure it in place with a few pins.

5. Using a thread color that matches the plush, machine stitch around the appliqué, about ⅛" from the raw edge.

APPLIQUÉ THE NEEDLE-TURN WAY

Although there are several different ways to appliqué, this is the method my mother taught me. With this technique, a freezer-paper template is pressed onto the right side of the fabric and used as a guide for turning the seam allowance under as you stitch the appliqué in place. This method ensures that the appliqué shape is stable and durable, adding to the lifetime of the appliqué.

Follow these steps for needle-turn appliqué:

1. Using a fine-line pencil, trace your appliqué shape onto the dull side of a piece of freezer paper. Do not add a seam allowance. Do not reverse the appliqué shape; trace it just as the finished appliqué will appear.

2. Cut out the shape on the drawn line.

3. Place the freezer-paper shape on the *right* side of the chosen fabric and press with a hot iron.

4. Cut out the appliqué shape, adding a ¼" seam allowance all around the freezer-paper shape. Clip the seam allowance on the inside corners as needed, stopping two or three threads from the freezer-paper shape.

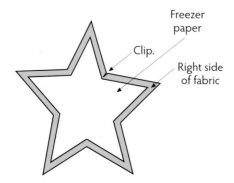

Freezer paper

Clip.

Right side of fabric

5. Place the appliqué on the background fabric. Pin the appliqué in place, placing the pins in the middle of the piece so the edges can easily be turned under.

6. Turn a portion of the seam allowance under until it's even with the edge of the freezer paper. Using a thread color that matches the appliqué piece, knot the end of the thread and secure it in the seam allowance. Insert the needle in the background fabric underneath the appliqué piece and come up through the background fabric about ⅛" away; with the tip of the needle, catch just the edge of the appliqué and pull the stitch taut. Using short stitches, about ⅛" long, continue this process unit your piece is completely stitched in place.

7. Remove the freezer paper.

Embellishing Your Quilt

What makes the baby quilts in this book really come to life is the little details you can add—from embroidery stitches to rickrack, buttons, and more.

EMBROIDERY

I added an embroidered monogram to "Gift-Wrapped" on page 75 as a tribute to my grandma Jessie. My grandmother could make some of the most beautiful hand stitches you can imagine, and with a lot of practice, I hope to be just as good someday. A great place to start learning embroidery is with the basic stem stitch.

Follow these instructions to make a stem stitch:

1. Using a fine-line pencil on light fabrics, or a white pencil on dark fabrics, trace the line you want to embroider on the right side of the fabric.

2. Thread an embroidery needle with two strands of embroidery floss. Cut lengths of embroidery floss approximately 18" long to avoid fraying and tangling the floss.

3. Knot one end of the embroidery floss. Bring the needle up through the fabric at A and pull the thread taut. Insert the needle at B and bring it up at C, pulling the thread taut.

4. Insert the needle at D, and continue stitching in this manner until you reach the end of the design line. Knot the thread on the wrong side of the fabric.

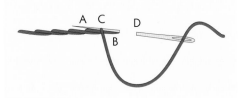

EYES

Two of the quilts in this book have cute little animals on them: "Twinkle, Twinkle" on page 17 has a plush polar bear and "Swimming Lessons" on page 45 has a cheery duck. And of course these animals need eyes!

I worked a long time on the bear's eye. At first I carefully cut a small circle and appliquéd it in place. However, it turned out less than perfect no matter how many times I tried.

The quickest solution to the bear's eye is to sew on a button. But I have a very strong warning. *Do not sew buttons onto any quilt where a small child or baby will be able to get hold of them.* Small babies can be scratched by the buttons, or even chew them off and choke on them. So please remember, if small children will be around these quilts, *no* buttons!

Here's a child-safe solution. I drew the size of eye I wanted onto the bear *after* it was appliquéd onto the quilt. Then I simply stitched the eye with my sewing machine and dark-brown thread! I outlined the eye first, and then filled it in by sewing back and forth across the shape until it was filled with thread. This gave me the perfectly round eye that I wanted, which could not be pulled off by little hands. So if you encounter frustration appliquéing little eyes, you may want to try this technique. It worked so well, I used this technique on the duck's eye as well.

RICKRACK

When I first saw the new wide rickrack in stores, I was thrilled! It instantly took me back to my days before kindergarten, when I would play in the drawers of my mother's sewing cabinet. I loved the ribbons and trims, and when I found a piece of rickrack, I thought I had struck gold. So I naturally wanted to include this beloved trim on some of these projects, so that a new generation can begin its love affair with this great trim.

What's wonderful about this rickrack is that it makes a big impact and it's easy to use. You'll see it used in two of the quilts in this book: "Twinkle, Twinkle" on page 17 and "Birthday Bash" on page 41.

To add rickrack to your quilts:

1. Pin the rickrack securely in place.

2. Using a thread color that matches the rickrack, sew along each side of the rickrack, close to the edge. (I use a free-motion darning foot, which makes it easy to sew along the wavy lines of the trim.) If you only sew through the center, the edges will curl up and won't want to lay flat.

Details of the giant rickrack used in "Twinkle, Twinkle" and "Birthday Bash."

MONOGRAMS

I love monograms. I think my obsession began when I was almost a teenager and I got my first monogrammed sweater. It was preppy, it was trendy, and it was a rare plum-rose color. I still have that sweater, and I still remember the pride I felt when wearing it. Now, I've brought that same feeling to some of the projects in this book. Adding a personal monogram shows that you didn't make a quilt for just anyone, but rather that you spent time creating a quilt for someone extra special.

Here are some tips for adding monograms.

Choosing a font. Picking a font for your monogram is like adding personality to your quilt. There are so many choices. Do you want it to be fun and frilly? Or do you want it to be strong and stoic? When picking a font, I tend to use flowing script on a girl's quilt and a more traditional font on a boy's quilt; however, the possibilities are almost endless. You'll probably find a wide variety of fonts available in the word-processing program on your computer. When you pick a font, keep in mind the ends and the curves of each letter. You may find it difficult to appliqué a letter that has thin or pointy ends or narrow curves. I find it easiest to work with letters that have roughly the same width throughout the shape. You can modify the letters as needed to achieve a consistent width. One of my favorite fonts is called Engravers.

Font size. The size of your font will depend on how many letters you're using and the space the letters need to fill. A quick rule of thumb is to have the monogram fill about three-quarters of the background area. You can test the shape and size of the letters by printing them on paper, cutting them out, and pinning them in place on your project. Take a few steps back and see if the size and shape feel balanced. For the letter *S* in "Sandbox" on page 27 and shown above, I wasn't able to print a letter from my computer that was as large as I needed, so I used a photocopier to enlarge the letter enough to fill the square.

Text direction. When creating your monogram templates, keep in mind which appliqué or embroidery technique you're planning to use. If you're using the "Appliqué the Plush Way" technique on page 7, you'll need to reverse your letters before cutting them out of the fabric. If you need to make a reversed image, print the letter onto a piece of paper; then place the paper on a light box or against a bright window, with the printed side toward the window. Trace the letter onto the back of the paper using a permanent pen.

Templates. Once you've determined the font you want to use, the size of the font, and the appliqué method, print the letter(s) onto paper to make a template. Cut out the template(s) and use it to cut the letter from the appropriate fabric.

Finishing Your Quilt

The end is certainly in sight. Now it's time to layer the quilt top with batting and backing, quilt the layers, and bind the edges. I've included quilting suggestions for each project, but I encourage you to use a design that fits your quilt and the recipient.

BASTING

Before you layer the quilt, carefully press the quilt top and backing. Then spread the backing wrong side up on a flat, clean surface. Anchor the backing with masking tape, taking care not to stretch the fabric out of shape. Center the batting over the backing, smoothing out any wrinkles. Center the quilt top, right side up, over the batting, again smoothing out any wrinkles. Baste the layers with #2 rustproof safety pins. Place the pins 4" to 6" apart. Remove the tape. Finish by machine basting around the edges about ⅛" from the edge of the quilt top.

Quilt top
Batting
Backing
Basting
Safety pins
Masking tape

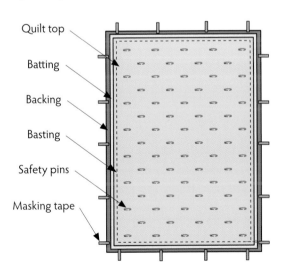

QUILTING

Quilting is what holds the sandwich of fabric and batting together. Traditionally quilting was done by hand, rocking a needle back and forth through all of the layers. Today, quilting is usually done using a sewing machine, which makes the task quicker and allows for more intricate patterns.

To quilt using a domestic sewing machine, I recommend using two different types of sewing-machine feet. To quilt straight lines, like in "Jack's Boxes" on page 71, I suggest using a walking foot. This foot helps compress the layers and move them evenly through the machine, which helps prevent bunching and pulling. If you want to quilt a design that flows over the entire quilt (see "Birthday Bash" on page 41), you'll need to use a darning foot. Depending on your sewing-machine model, you'll have a darning foot that's either *open toe* or a fully closed round foot. A darning foot allows you to freely move the fabric in various directions so you can quilt circles and swirls, hence the name *free-motion quilting*.

BINDING

When you've finished quilting your project, use a cutting mat, ruler, and rotary cutter to trim your quilt to its finished size. Trim each side so that all three layers (the quilt top, batting, and backing) have straight edges. Now you just need to add a binding or edging to finish the project.

There are a number of ways to bind the edge of your quilt. I prefer to finish my quilts using a double-fold binding made with strips cut 2½" wide and sewn with a ¼" seam allowance. Cut the required number of strips as instructed for the project.

1. Place two strips at right angles, right sides together. Draw a diagonal line on the top strip and stitch along the line as shown.

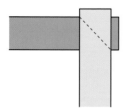

2. Trim the seam allowance to ¼". Press the seam allowances open. Add the remaining strips in the same manner to make one long strip.

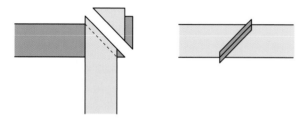

3. When all of the strips have been joined, cut one end at a 45° angle. This will be the beginning of the strip. Press the strip in half lengthwise, wrong sides together and raw edges aligned.

4. Beginning with the angled end, place the binding strip along one edge of the front of the quilt. Starting several inches away from a corner, align the raw edges of the strip with the quilt-top edge. Leaving the first 8" of the binding unstitched, use a ¼" seam allowance to stitch the binding to the quilt. Stop stitching ¼" from the corner and backstitch.

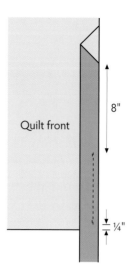

Quilt front

8"

¼"

5. Remove the quilt from the sewing machine. Turn the quilt so you're ready to sew the binding to the next side. Fold the binding straight up, away from the quilt, to create a 45°-angle fold. Fold the binding back down onto itself, even with the edge of the quilt top, to create an angled pleat at the corner. Beginning at the edge, stitch the binding to the quilt, stopping ¼" from the next corner. Repeat the process on the remaining corners of the quilt.

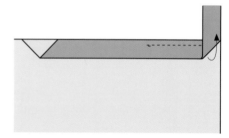

6. When you're 8" to 12" away from your starting point, stop stitching and remove the quilt from the machine. Cut the end of the binding strip so it overlaps the beginning of the binding strip by at least 5". Pin the ends together 3½" from the starting point. Clip the binding raw edges at the pin, being careful not to cut past the seam allowance or into the quilt layers. Open up the binding and match the clipped edges as shown, right sides together. Stitch the binding strips together on the diagonal.

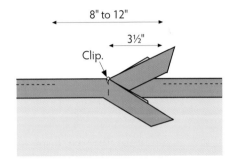

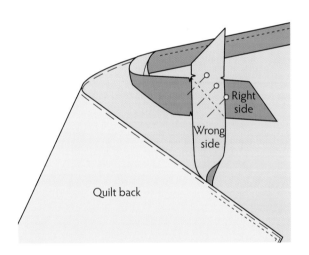

7. Refold the binding and check to make sure it fits the quilt. Trim the binding ends, leaving a ¼" seam allowance. Press the seam allowances open. Finish stitching the binding to the quilt top.

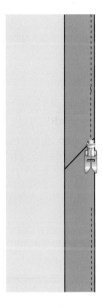

8. Fold the binding to the back of the quilt. Using matching thread and making sure the machine stitching line is covered, hand stitch the folded edge to the backing. Fold the binding to form a miter at each corner.

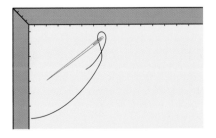

"Twinkle, Twinkle," pieced and appliquéd by Myra Harder; quilted by Katie Friesen

Twinkle, Twinkle

QUILT SIZE: 35½" x 41½"

When the stars come out at night, everything becomes quiet, and we tuck ourselves in for a peaceful rest. But this little polar bear has decided to explore the night to discover how the stars are hung in the sky.

MATERIALS

Yardage is based on 42"-wide cotton fabric and 60"-wide plush fabric.

1⅓ yards of light-blue print cotton for border and binding
¾ yard of medium-blue print cotton for background
¼ yard of yellow plush fabric for stars
½ yard of white plush fabric for polar bear
1⅓ yards of fabric for backing
40" x 46" piece of batting
1 yard of 1"-wide rickrack for stars

CUTTING

The star patterns are on pages 19 and 20. The polar bear pattern is on pages 20–22. Assemble the full-sized polar bear pattern and refer to "Appliqué the Plush Way" on page 7.

From the medium-blue print, cut:
1 square, 25½" x 25½"

From the light-blue print, cut:
2 strips, 5½" x 25½"
1 strip, 5½" x 35½"
1 strip, 11½" x 35½"
5 strips, 2½" x 42"

From the white plush, cut:
1 polar bear

From the yellow plush, cut:
1 large star
1 medium star
1 small star

From the rickrack, cut:
1 piece, 12½" long
1 piece, 9½" long
1 piece, 7½" long

ASSEMBLING THE QUILT TOP

1. Sew light-blue 5½" x 25½" strips to opposite sides of the medium-blue square. Press the seam allowances toward the light-blue strips.

2. Sew the light-blue 5½" x 35½" strip to the top of the medium-blue square. Then sew the light-blue 11½" x 35½" strip to the bottom of the square to complete the border. Press the seam allowances toward the light-blue strips.

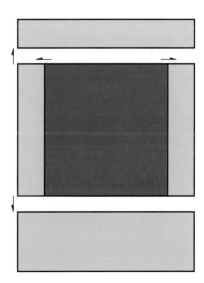

3. Position the polar bear in the lower-right corner of the medium-blue square, with the feet and hindquarters slightly overlapping the light-blue border. Refer to the photo on page 16 and the diagram below for placement guidance. Appliqué the polar bear in place. Add the eye detail, referring to "Eyes" on page 9 as needed.

4. In the upper-left corner of the quilt top, place the 12½"-long piece of rickrack 6½" in from the left edge of the quilt top and stitch in place, referring to "Rickrack" on page 10. Appliqué the large star to the end of the rickrack.

5. Position the 7½"-long piece of rickrack 1½" to the right of the first hanging star and stitch in place. Appliqué the small star to the end of the rickrack.

6. Position the 9½"-long piece of rickrack 2½" to the right of the middle hanging star and stitch in place. Appliqué the medium star to the end of the rickrack.

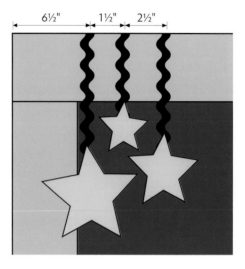

FINISHING THE QUILT

For detailed instructions on finishing techniques, refer to "Finishing Your Quilt" on page 13.

1. Cut and piece the backing fabric so it's 3" to 6" larger than the quilt top. Layer the quilt top with batting and backing. Baste the layers together.

2. Hand or machine quilt as desired.

3. Square up the quilt sandwich.

4. Use the light-blue 2½"-wide strips to make and attach the binding.

> ✤ **Quilting Suggestions**
>
> "Twinkle, Twinkle" gives you a great opportunity to use quilting lines to suggest wind. Fill in the background area with tight swirls of wind; use larger swirls to cover the border. Adding the movement of wind to the quilt will help it to feel fun and carefree.

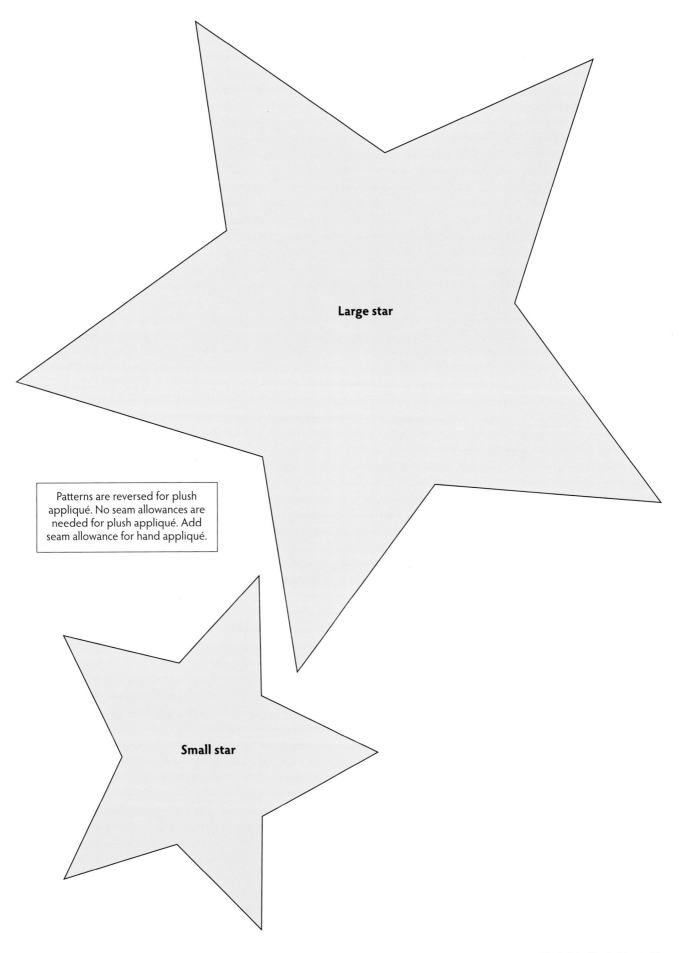

Large star

Patterns are reversed for plush appliqué. No seam allowances are needed for plush appliqué. Add seam allowance for hand appliqué.

Small star

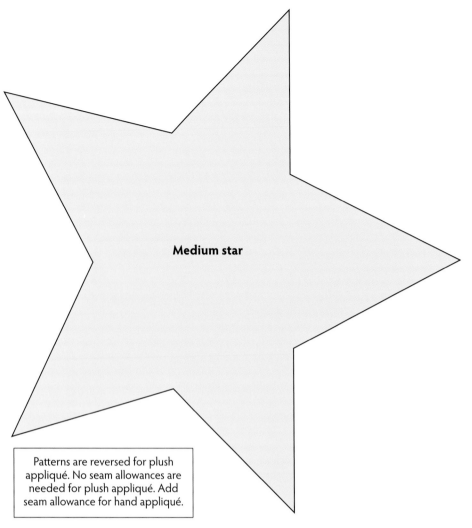

Medium star

Patterns are reversed for plush appliqué. No seam allowances are needed for plush appliqué. Add seam allowance for hand appliqué.

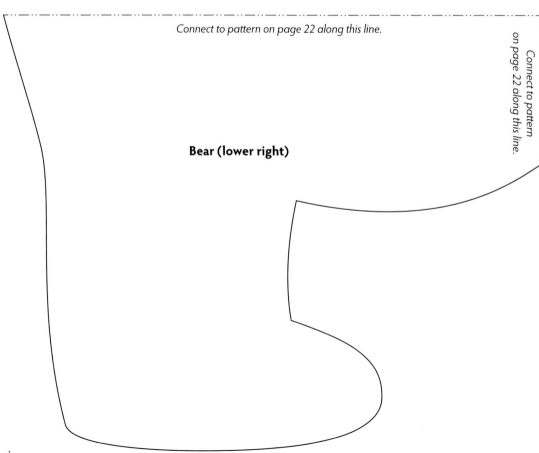

Connect to pattern on page 22 along this line.

Connect to pattern on page 22 along this line.

Bear (lower right)

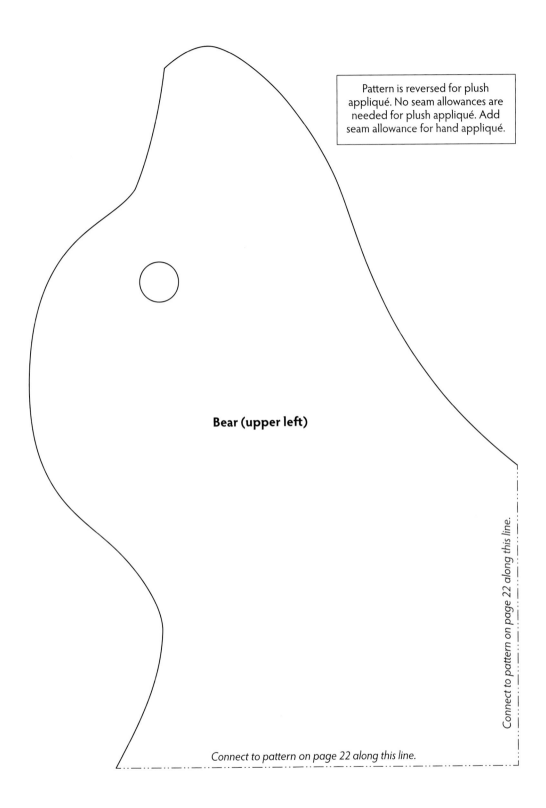

Pattern is reversed for plush appliqué. No seam allowances are needed for plush appliqué. Add seam allowance for hand appliqué.

Bear (upper left)

Connect to pattern on page 22 along this line.

Connect to pattern on page 22 along this line.

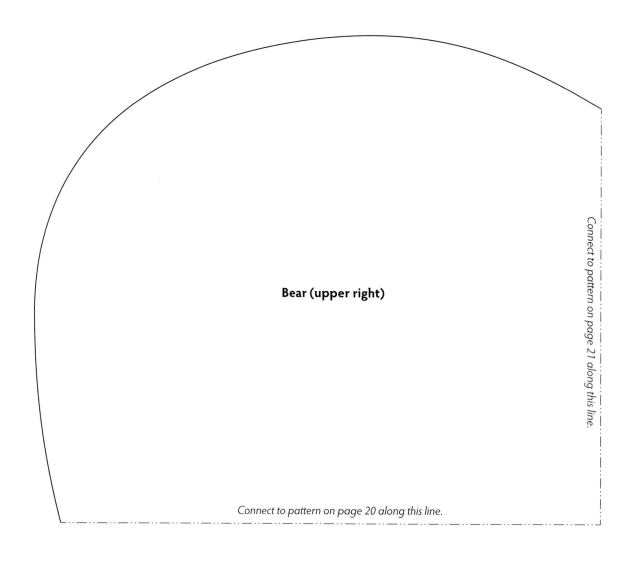

Bear (upper right)

Connect to pattern on page 21 along this line.

Connect to pattern on page 20 along this line.

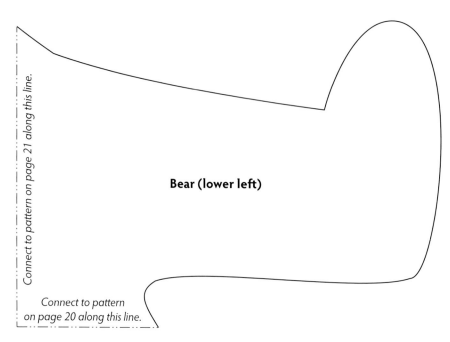

Bear (lower left)

Connect to pattern on page 21 along this line.

Connect to pattern on page 20 along this line.

Playpen

A playpen is a bright and fun place. In it, Baby finds her favorite toys and a soft place to rest, and can sometimes even share the space with little friends who drop by. This quilt would be a perfect addition to any time spent in a playpen.

MATERIALS

Yardage is based on 42"-wide fabric.

¼ yard *each* of 8 assorted prints *OR* 15 strips, 2½" x 42", for blocks
1¼ yards of light print for blocks
½ yard of green print for binding
2⅜ yards of fabric for backing*
41" x 53" piece of batting
Template plastic

If the backing fabric measures 42" wide after washing and trimming off the selvages, you can use a single width, 1⅝ yards long.

CUTTING

From the assorted prints, cut a *total* of:
15 strips, 2½" x 42"

From the light print, cut:
15 strips, 2½" x 42"

From the green print, cut:
5 strips, 2½" x 42"

MAKING THE BLOCKS

1. Join assorted print strips to both long edges of a light strip to make strip set A. Press the seam allowances toward the assorted print strips. Make a total of five strip sets.

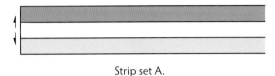

Strip set A.
Make 5.

2. Join light strips to both long edges of an assorted print strip to make strip set B. Press the seam allowances toward the assorted print strip. Make a total of five strip sets.

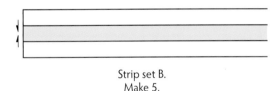

Strip set B.
Make 5.

3. Referring to "Making a Template" on page 37, trace the triangle pattern on page 26 onto template plastic, making sure to trace the lines exactly. Cut out the template on the drawn lines.

4. Using the template, cut out five triangle units from each strip set as shown. Cut a total of 24 triangle units from the A strip sets and 24 triangle units from the B strip sets. (You'll have one extra triangle unit from each group of strip sets.)

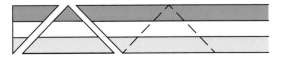

"Playpen," pieced by Myra Harder; quilted by Katie Friesen

5. Lay out two strip set A triangle units and two strip set B triangle units as shown. Join the units into pairs. Press the seam allowances in the directions indicated. Join the pairs to make a block. Press the seam allowances in one direction. Make a total of 12 blocks.

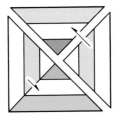 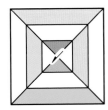

ASSEMBLING THE QUILT TOP

1. Lay out the blocks in four rows of three blocks each, rotating every other block as shown in the quilt assembly diagram below.

2. Join the blocks into rows. Press the seam allowances in opposite directions from row to row. Join the rows and press the seam allowances in one direction.

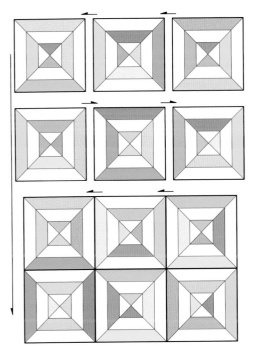

Quilt assembly

FINISHING THE QUILT

For detailed instructions on finishing techniques, refer to "Finishing Your Quilt" on page 13.

1. Cut and piece the backing fabric so it's 3" to 6" larger than the quilt top. Layer the quilt top with batting and backing. Baste the layers together.

2. Hand or machine quilt as desired.

3. Square up the quilt sandwich.

4. Use the green 2½"-wide strips to make and attach the binding.

> ❖ **Quilting Suggestions**
>
> "Playpen" was quilted using a traditional Greek key design on the white fabric only, which allowed the printed fabric to really pop! I think it's a great way to add the perfect detail to the quilt.

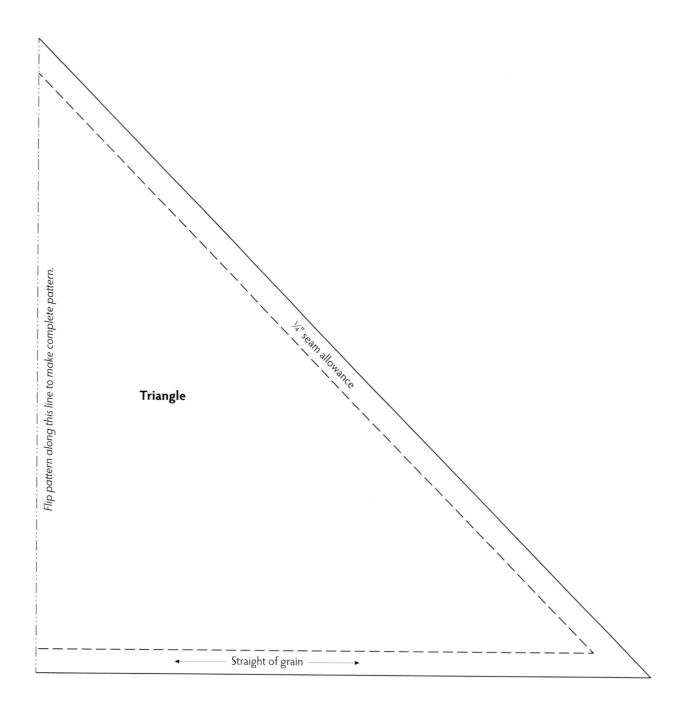

Triangle

Flip pattern along this line to make complete pattern.

¼" seam allowance

Straight of grain

Sandbox

Little kids love to play in sandboxes. A sandbox is a place to dig and explore and to feel the sand fall through your fingers. I hope you'll have just as much fun playing with this sandbox, where you can add the initial of someone very special.

MATERIALS

Yardage is based on 42"-wide fabric.

1⅞ yards of light-teal print for blocks, sashing, border, and binding

½ yard of green print for blocks

½ yard of white print for blocks

½ yard of dark-teal print for block centers and letter

1½ yards of fabric for backing

40" x 51" piece of batting

CUTTING

Refer to "Monograms" on page 11 to make a letter pattern. Refer to "Appliqué the Needle-Turn Way" on page 8.

From the light-teal print, cut:

1 square, 16½" x 16½"

14 strips, 2½" x 42"; crosscut *5 of the strips* into:

    2 strips, 2½" x 35½"

    1 strip, 2½" x 22½"

    7 strips, 2½" x 9½"

4 strips, 1½" x 42"; crosscut into:

    16 strips, 1½" x 5½"

    16 strips, 1½" x 3½"

From the dark-teal print, cut:

8 squares, 3½" x 3½"

Letter of your choice

From the white print, cut:

8 strips, 1½" x 42"; crosscut into:

    2 strips, 1½" x 18½"

    2 strips, 1½" x 16½"

    16 strips, 1½" x 7½"

    16 strips, 1½" x 5½"

From the green print, cut:

10 strips, 1½" x 42"; crosscut into:

    2 strips, 1½" x 20½"

    2 strips, 1½" x 18½"

    16 strips, 1½" x 9½"

    16 strips, 1½" x 7½"

MAKING THE PIECED BLOCKS

1. Sew light-teal 1½" x 3½" strips to opposite sides of a dark-teal square. Press the seam allowances toward the light-teal strips. Sew light-teal 1½" x 5½" strips to the top and bottom of the square. Press the seam allowances toward the light-teal strips. Make a total of eight units.

Make 8.

"Sandbox," pieced and appliquéd by Myra Harder; quilted by Katie Friesen

2. Sew white 1½" x 5½" strips to opposite sides of a unit from step 1. Press the seam allowances toward the white strips. Sew white 1½" x 7½" strips to the top and bottom of the unit. Press the seam allowances toward the white strips. Make a total of eight units.

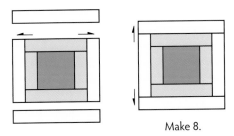

Make 8.

3. Sew green 1½" x 7½" strips to opposite sides of a unit from step 2. Press the seam allowances toward the green strips. Sew green 1½" x 9½" strips to the top and bottom of the unit to complete the block. Press the seam allowances toward the green strips. The block should measure 9½" square. Make a total of eight blocks.

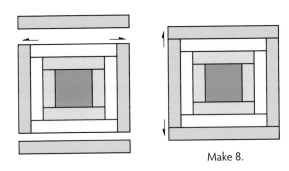

Make 8.

MAKING THE APPLIQUÉD BLOCK

1. Sew white 1½" x 16½" strips to opposite sides of the light-teal 16½" square. Press the seam allowances toward the white strips. Sew white 1½" x 18½" strips to the top and bottom of the square. Press the seam allowances toward the white strips.

2. Sew green 1½" x 18½" strips to opposite sides of the unit from step 1. Press the seam allowances toward the green strips. Sew green 1½" x 20½" strips to the top and bottom of the

unit to complete the block. Press the seam allowances toward the green strips. The block should measure 20½" square.

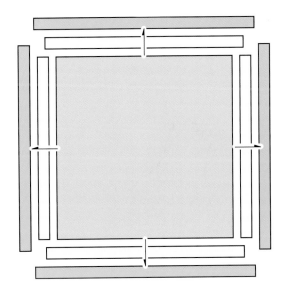

✣ **Time to Appliqué**
Monogramming is a great way to add your personal touch to the appliquéd block. You'll find it easier to add the appliquéd letter to the large block *before* assembling the quilt.

3. Position the appliqué letter in the center of the block. Appliqué in place.

ASSEMBLING THE QUILT TOP

1. Join two pieced blocks and two light-teal 2½" x 9½" strips to make a vertical row as shown. Press the seam allowances toward the light-teal strips. Make two vertical rows.

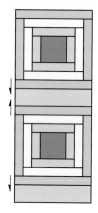

Make 2.

2. Sew the vertical rows to opposite sides of the light-teal 2½" x 22½" strip as shown. Press the seam allowances toward the light-teal strip.

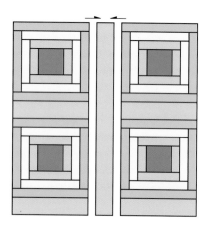

3. Sew the appliquéd block to the bottom of the section from step 2 as shown above right to make a vertical row. Press the seam allowances toward the appliquéd block.

4. Join four pieced blocks and the remaining light-teal 2½" x 9½" strips to make a vertical row as shown. Press the seam allowances toward the light-teal strips.

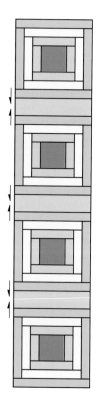

5. Join four light-teal 2½" x 42" strips end to end. From the pieced strip, cut three 42½"-long strips. Lay out the strips and the vertical rows from steps 3 and 4 as shown. Join the pieces and press the seam allowances toward the light-teal strips.

6. Sew the light-teal 2½" x 35½" strips to the top and bottom edges to complete the quilt top. Press the seam allowances toward the light-teal strips.

FINISHING THE QUILT

For detailed instructions on finishing techniques, refer to "Finishing Your Quilt" on page 13.

1. Cut and piece the backing fabric so it's 3" to 6" larger than the quilt top. Layer the quilt top with batting and backing. Baste the layers together.

2. Hand or machine quilt as desired.

3. Square up the quilt sandwich.

4. Use the remaining light-teal 2½"-wide strips to make and attach the binding.

> ❧ *Quilting Suggestions*
>
> There are several creative ways to quilt "Sandbox." A traditional style would be to outline quilt in each round of the pieced blocks. However, Katie and I decided to try a different idea. Just like sand that doesn't stay in the sandbox, the quilting flows out of the box. A large motif is quilted over each of the eight pieced blocks, and a meandering line is quilted in the background of the appliquéd block to make the letter stand out. Finally, the sashing and border are quilted with a swirl that winds between the boxes.

"Gummy Bears," made and appliquéd by Myra Harder; quilted by Katie Friesen

Gummy Bears

QUILT SIZE: 34½" x 42½"

Who can resist a soft, sugary treat? This bright and fun quilt is also irresistible. And by using plush fabrics, this quilt will come together faster than eating a handful of gummy bears.

MATERIALS

Yardage is based on 42"-wide cotton fabric and 60"-wide plush fabric.

1¼ yards of white print cotton for background
⅜ yard *each* of 3 plush fabrics (green, red, orange) for bears
½ yard of orange polka-dot cotton for binding
1⅜ yards of fabric for backing
39" x 47" piece of batting

CUTTING

The bear pattern is on pages 34 and 35. Assemble the full-sized pattern and refer to "Appliqué the Plush Way" on page 7.

From *each* of the 3 plush fabrics, cut:
2 bears (6 total)

From the orange polka dot, cut:
5 strips, 2½" x 42"

ASSEMBLING THE QUILT TOP

Referring to the photo on page 32 and the diagram below for placement guidance, position the bears in various directions on the white background. The quilt will be trimmed after it's quilted (approximately 2" from each side and 1" from the top and bottom edges), so be aware of how much of each bear will be cut off. Appliqué the bears in place.

FINISHING THE QUILT

For detailed instructions on finishing techniques, refer to "Finishing Your Quilt" on page 13.

1. Cut and piece the backing fabric so it's 3" to 6" larger than the quilt top. Layer the quilt top with batting and backing. Baste the layers together.

2. Hand or machine quilt as desired.

3. Square up the quilt sandwich.

4. Use the orange polka-dot 2½"-wide strips to make and attach the binding.

❖ **Quilting Suggestions**

Have as much fun quilting this project as you did creating it. Use an overall design that's large and cheerful to cover the quilt. The quilting adds stability and fun to this happy quilt.

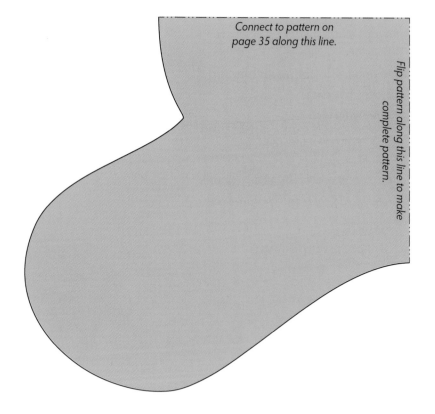

Connect to pattern on page 35 along this line.

Flip pattern along this line to make complete pattern.

No seam allowances are
needed for plush appliqué.
Add seam allowance for
hand appliqué.

Pattern assembly

Bear
Make 6.

Flip pattern along this line to make complete pattern.

*Connect to pattern on
page 34 along this line.*

"Picking Pansies," pieced by Myra Harder; quilted by Katie Friesen

Picking Pansies

QUILT SIZE: 31½" x 45½"

Little children love picking flowers. When they see a beautiful flower, they naturally want to pluck it and give it to someone special. With this traditional quilt, you can pick your favorite fabrics and wrap them around your little one.

MATERIALS

Yardage is based on 42"-wide fabric.

⅞ yard of teal print for flower centers and binding
⅔ yard *each* of navy, purple, green, and light-blue prints for flowers
1½ yards of fabric for backing
36" x 49" piece of batting
Template plastic

CUTTING

Referring to "Making a Template," right, make a plastic template of the hexagon pattern on page 40 for cutting the fabric pieces.

From the teal print, cut:
11 hexagons
5 strips, 2½" x 42"

From the navy print, cut:
15 hexagons

From the purple print, cut:
18 hexagons

From the green print, cut:
21 hexagons

From the light-blue print, cut:
15 hexagons

✤ *Making a Template*

To make a template, trace the pattern onto template plastic with a fine-tipped permanent pen, making sure to trace the lines exactly. All template patterns include seam allowances. Use utility scissors to cut out the template on the drawn line. When placing the template on the fabric, pay careful attention to the grain line noted on the template.

ASSEMBLING THE QUILT TOP

1. The quilt is assembled in eight vertical rows with 10 hexagons in each row. Lay out your hexagons in vertical rows as shown. Pay close attention to color placement; the strips will form flowers when sewn together.

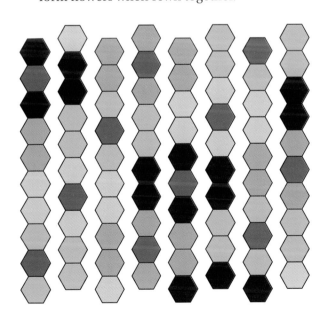

2. Join the hexagons in each row, beginning and ending ¼" from both ends of the hexagons with a backstitch.

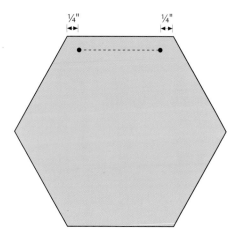

Backstitch ¼" from corners.

3. Lay out the first two rows from step 2, staggering them as shown in the quilt assembly diagram. Align the edge of the hexagon at the top of the first row with the edge of the hexagon in the second row. Join the hexagons, stopping ¼" from the corner of the hexagons. Pivot the second row to align the edges of the next two hexagons and sew the hexagons together, stopping ¼" from the corner. Continue in the same way to the end of the row, pivoting the second row to align the next two hexagons and stopping ¼" from the corner.

4. Repeat step 3 to join the remaining six rows to the first two rows as shown.

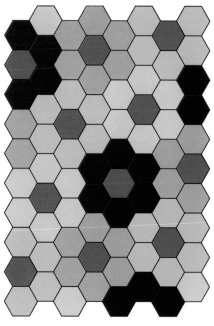

Quilt assembly

5. Using a ruler and rotary cutter, trim the sides, top, and bottom of the quilt top as shown.

FINISHING THE QUILT

For detailed instructions on finishing techniques, refer to "Finishing Your Quilt" on page 13.

1. Cut and piece the backing fabric so it's 3" to 6" larger than the quilt top. Layer the quilt top with batting and backing. Baste the layers together.

2. Hand or machine quilt as desired.

3. Square up the quilt sandwich.

4. Use the teal 2½"-wide strips to make and attach the binding.

❖ Quilting Suggestions

The hexagons were outline quilted ¼" from the seam lines to tie the fabrics and flowers together. Another option would be to quilt a motif in the flower centers, giving the quilt a unique design.

"Hexagons," pieced and quilted by Myra Harder

❖ Alternate Layout

If you like a less formal garden, this quilt is a great place to use your scraps, giving a completely different look to the very same design. You'll need a total of 2¼ yards of scrap fabrics. Cut 80 hexagons using the pattern on page 40. Lay out the hexagons in vertical columns as for the main quilt, disregarding color—placement is totally random. Sew the hexagons together in the same manner and trim the completed quilt in the same way.

A quilt with a random fabric design pairs perfectly with a large, wandering quilting motif. I quilted ¼" from the seam lines so the quilting zigzagged vertically down the quilt.

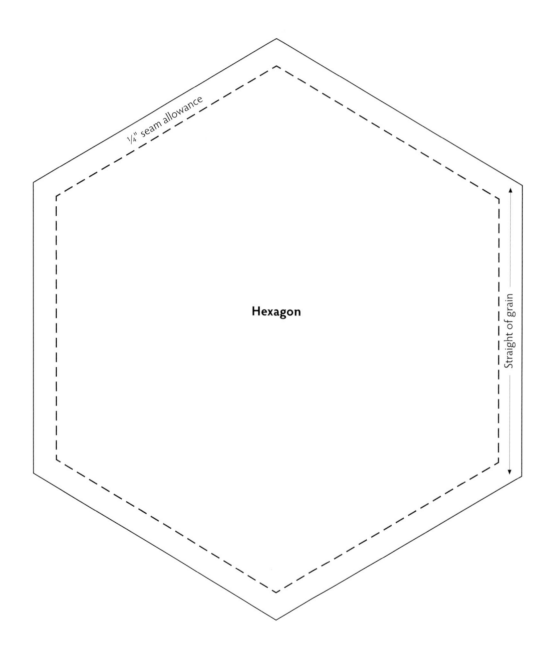

Hexagon

¼" seam allowance

Straight of grain

Birthday Bash

Planning a great birthday bash can be as much fun as attending one. Birthdays mark the milestones of the ones we love the most—definitely a reason to celebrate. This quilt will come together just as fast as hanging the streamers and making the cake.

MATERIALS

Yardage is based on 42"-wide fabric.

1⅓ yards of light print for background
7 squares, 8" x 8", of assorted prints for flags
½ yard of blue stripe for binding
1⅜ yards of fabric for backing
41" x 47" piece of batting
2½ yards of 1"-wide rickrack
Template plastic

CUTTING

Referring to "Making a Template" on page 37, make a plastic template of the A and B patterns on pages 43 and 44 for cutting the fabric pieces.

From the *lengthwise grain* of the light print, cut:
1 strip, 24½" x 42½"
1 strip, 6½" x 42½"

From the remaining light print, cut:
6 A triangles
1 B triangle
1 B reversed triangle

From the assorted prints, cut:
7 A triangles

From the blue stripe, cut:
5 strips, 2½" x 42"

ASSEMBLING THE QUILT TOP

1. Lay out the A triangles, alternating the assorted prints and lights and also alternating the orientation as shown to make a row. Sew the triangles together, offsetting the triangles as shown. Press the seam allowances toward the print triangles. Sew a B triangle to each end of the row and press. The row should measure 6½" x 42½".

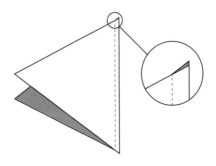

2. Sew the light 6½"-wide strip to the left side of the triangle row. Press the seam allowances toward the light strip. Sew the light 24½"-wide strip to the right side of the triangle row. Press the seam allowances toward the light strip.

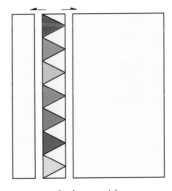

Quilt assembly

"Birthday Bash," pieced by Myra Harder; quilted by Katie Friesen

3. Cut the rickrack into two 45"-long pieces. Referring to "Rickrack" on page 10, sew the first strip of rickrack atop the seam line on the left side of the triangles. Position the second piece of rickrack approximately 1" to the left of the first piece, aligning the waves to match the first piece, and sew in place. Trim the ends of the rickrack even with the edge of the quilt top.

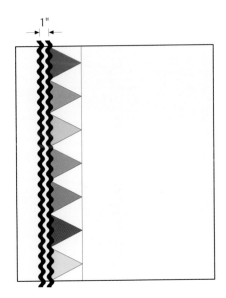

FINISHING THE QUILT

For detailed instructions on finishing techniques, refer to "Finishing Your Quilt" on page 13.

1. Cut and piece the backing fabric so it's 3" to 6" larger than the quilt top. Layer the quilt top with batting and backing. Baste the layers together.

2. Hand or machine quilt as desired.

3. Square up the quilt sandwich.

4. Use the blue-striped 2½"-wide strips to make and attach the binding.

✤ Quilting Suggestions

An overall design of swirls and lines was quilted in the background to imitate wind and keep the flags flying. You can decide if you want to quilt a gently rolling breeze or a full swirling winter wind. The large open area is also a great place to quilt the name of someone special.

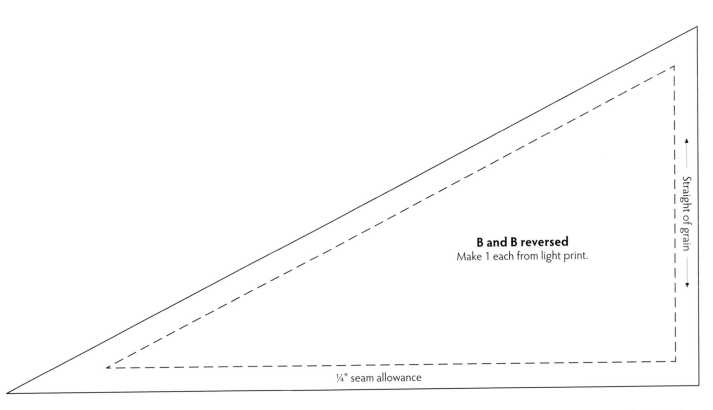

B and B reversed
Make 1 each from light print.

Straight of grain

¼" seam allowance

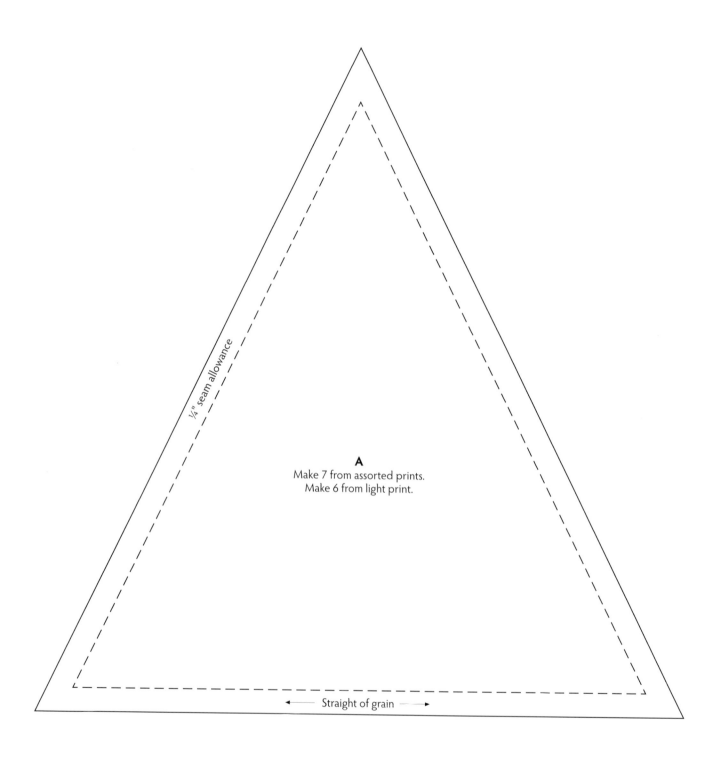

A
Make 7 from assorted prints.
Make 6 from light print.

¼" seam allowance

Straight of grain

Swimming Lessons

*S*plashing in the water can make us smile and laugh all day long. This bright quilt will remind you of summer fun no matter the season.

MATERIALS

Yardage is based on 42"-wide cotton fabric.

1⅝ yards of white print cotton for background

⅝ yard of green polka-dot cotton for border and binding

⅓ yard of blue print cotton for zigzags

14" x 14" square of green plush fabric for ring

7" x 7" square of yellow plush fabric for duck

2" x 2" square of orange plush fabric for beak

1⅓ yards of fabric for backing

39" x 45" piece of batting

CUTTING

Patterns for the ring and circle are on pages 50 and 51. The duck and beak patterns are on page 49. Refer to "Appliqué the Plush Way" on page 7.

From the white print, cut:

1 strip, 24½" x 32½"

1 strip, 6½" x 32½"

3 strips, 2⅞" x 42"; crosscut into 32 squares, 2⅞" x 2⅞"

1 circle

From the blue print, cut:

3 strips, 2⅞" x 42"; crosscut into 32 squares, 2⅞" x 2⅞"

From the green polka dot, cut:

2 strips, 1½" x 38½"

2 strips, 1½" x 34½"

4 strips, 2½" x 42"

From the green plush, cut:

1 ring

From the yellow plush, cut:

1 duck

From the orange plush, cut:

1 beak

"Swimming Lessons," pieced and appliquéd by Myra Harder; quilted by Katie Friesen

MAKING THE BLOCKS

Layer a white square right sides together with a blue square. Draw a diagonal line from corner to corner on the wrong side of the white square. Sew ¼" from both sides of the marked line. Cut the squares apart on the drawn line to make two half-square-triangle units. Press the seam allowances toward the blue triangle. The units should measure 2½" square. Make a total of 64 half-square-triangle units.

ASSEMBLING THE QUILT TOP

1. Lay out the half-square-triangle units in four rows of 16 units each, rotating the units as shown. Sew the units together in rows. Press the seam allowances in opposite directions from row to row. Join the rows to make a zigzag strip. Press the seam allowances in one direction.

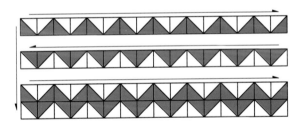

2. Join the white 24½" x 32½" strip, the zigzag strip, and the white 6½" x 32½" strip as shown in the quilt assembly diagram at right. Press the seam allowances toward the white strips.

3. Sew green 38½"-long strips to opposite sides of the quilt top. Press the seam allowances toward the green strips. Sew green 34½"-long strips to the top and bottom of the quilt top. Press the seam allowances toward the green strips.

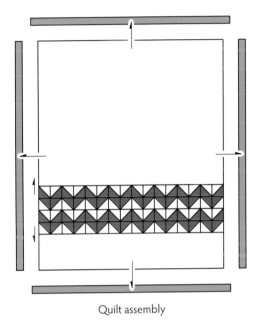

Quilt assembly

4. On the left side of the quilt, place the white circle atop the zigzag strip as shown. Sew the circle in place using a straight stitch. Don't worry about sewing a perfect circle; the green plush ring will cover the sewing lines.

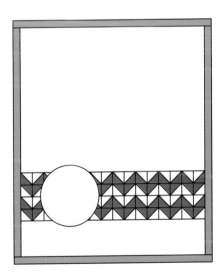

5. Place the green plush ring atop the white circle, covering all of the raw edges on the white circle. Appliqué in place.

6. Place the yellow plush duck in the center of the white circle, and then position the orange plush beak on the duck. Appliqué the shapes in place.

7. Machine stitch the eye detail, referring to "Eyes" on page 9.

FINISHING THE QUILT

For detailed instructions on finishing techniques, refer to "Finishing Your Quilt" on page 13.

1. Cut and piece the backing fabric so it's 3" to 6" larger than the quilt top. Layer the quilt top with batting and backing. Baste the layers together.

2. Hand or machine quilt as desired.

3. Square up the quilt sandwich.

4. Use the green polka-dot 2½"-wide strips to make and attach the binding.

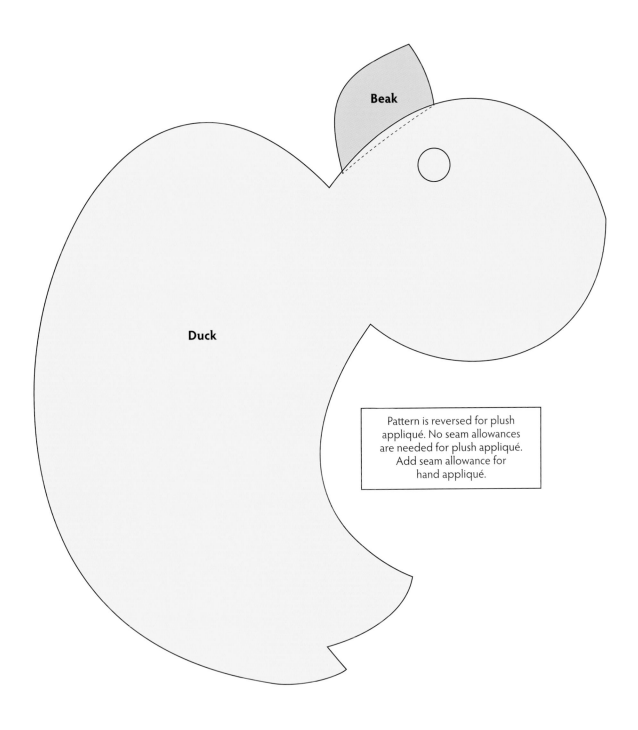

Beak

Duck

Pattern is reversed for plush
appliqué. No seam allowances
are needed for plush appliqué.
Add seam allowance for
hand appliqué.

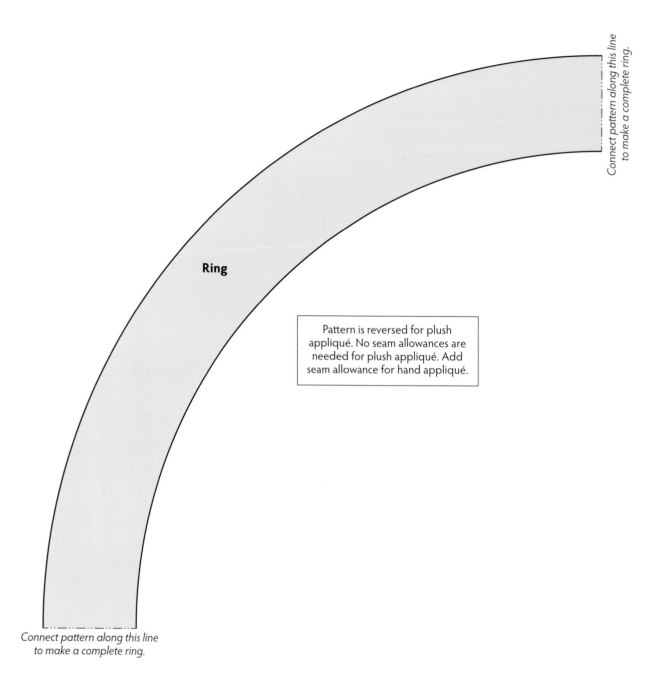

Ring

Pattern is reversed for plush appliqué. No seam allowances are needed for plush appliqué. Add seam allowance for hand appliqué.

Connect pattern along this line to make a complete ring.

Connect pattern along this line to make a complete ring.

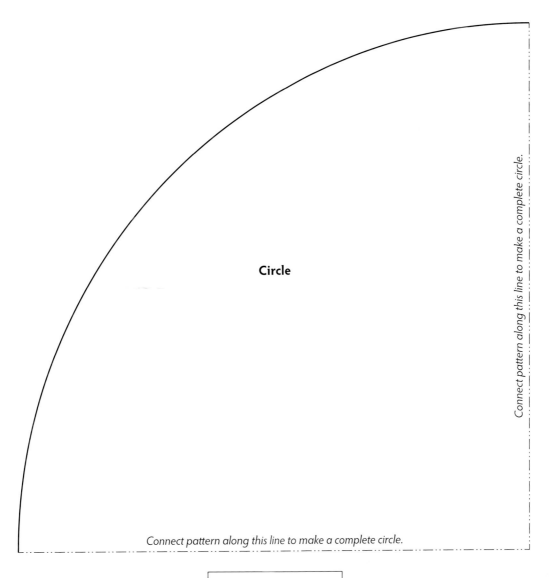

Circle

Connect pattern along this line to make a complete circle.

Connect pattern along this line to make a complete circle.

Pattern does not include
seam allowance.

"Gumdrops," pieced by Myra Harder; quilted by Katie Friesen

Gumdrops

Gumdrops are bright and cheerful, and always bring a smile. You'll get the same reaction when you make this fun little quilt for someone special. Simply pick your favorite colors and mix them together to make this sweet baby quilt.

MATERIALS

Yardage is based on 42"-wide fabric.

⅓ yard *each* of 6 assorted prints (red, green, orange, yellow, and blue) for blocks
⅔ yard of dark-red print for blocks and binding
½ yard of light print for border
3 yards of fabric for backing*
41" x 49" piece of batting
Template plastic

*If the backing fabric measures 42" wide after washing and trimming off the selvages, you can use a single width of 1½ yards.

CUTTING

Referring to "Making a Template" on page 37, make a plastic template of the A and B patterns on pages 55–57 for cutting the fabric pieces.

From the assorted prints, cut a *total* of:
17 A pieces
16 B pieces

From the dark-red print, cut:
5 strips, 2½" x 42"
3 A pieces
4 B pieces

From the light print, cut:
2 strips, 3½" x 38"
2 strips, 3½" x 36½"

MAKING THE BLOCKS

1. Fold the A and B pieces in half along the curved edges; finger-press the fold to mark the centers. Randomly place an A piece on top of a B piece, matching the outer edges and centers. Pin in place.

2. Sew the pieces together to make a block, carefully stretching or easing both fabrics as you sew the seam. Press the seam allowances toward the A piece. Make a total of 20 blocks.

Make 20.

ASSEMBLING THE QUILT TOP

1. Lay out the blocks in five rows of four blocks each, rotating the blocks as shown. Make sure each row begins with a block that's facing in the opposite direction of the previous row. Sew the blocks together into rows. Press the seam allowances in opposite directions from row to row. Join the rows and press the seam allowances in one direction.

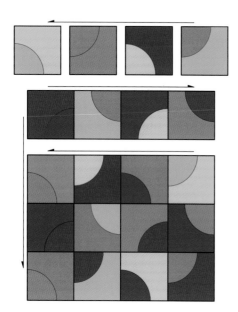

2. Sew the light 38"-long strips to opposite sides of the quilt top. Press the seam allowances toward the light strips. Sew the light 36½"-long strips to the top and bottom of the quilt top to complete the border. Press the seam allowances toward the light strips.

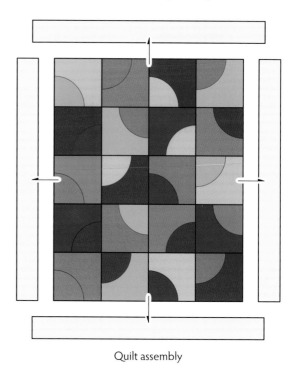

Quilt assembly

FINISHING THE QUILT

For detailed instructions on finishing techniques, refer to "Finishing Your Quilt" on page 13.

1. Cut and piece the backing fabric so it's 3" to 6" larger than the quilt top. Layer the quilt top with batting and backing. Baste the layers together.

2. Hand or machine quilt as desired.

3. Square up the quilt sandwich.

4. Use the dark-red 2½"-wide strips to make and attach the binding.

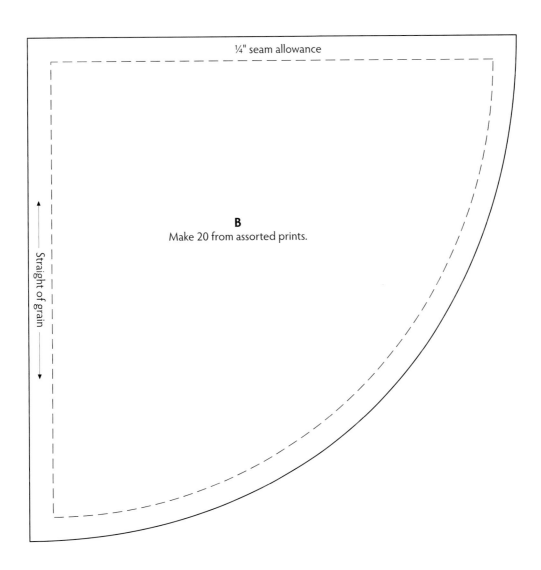

¼" seam allowance

Straight of grain

B
Make 20 from assorted prints.

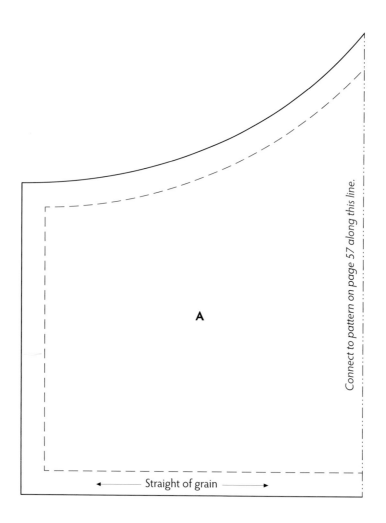

A

Connect to pattern on page 57 along this line.

Straight of grain

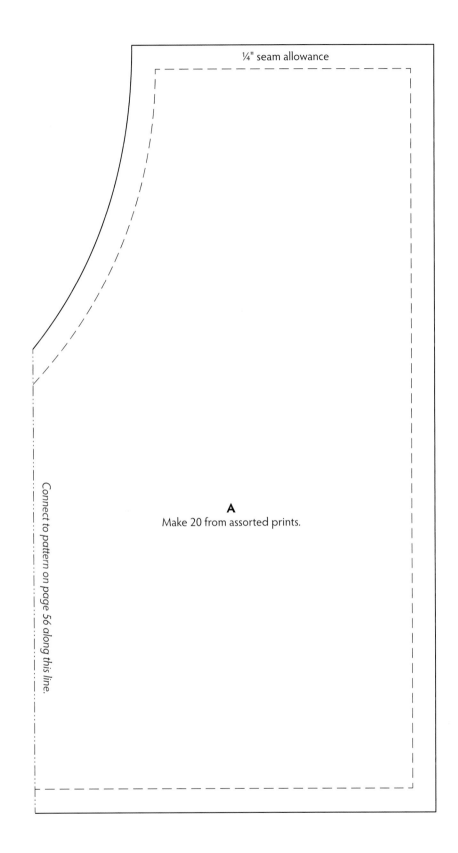

¼" seam allowance

A
Make 20 from assorted prints.

Connect to pattern on page 56 along this line.

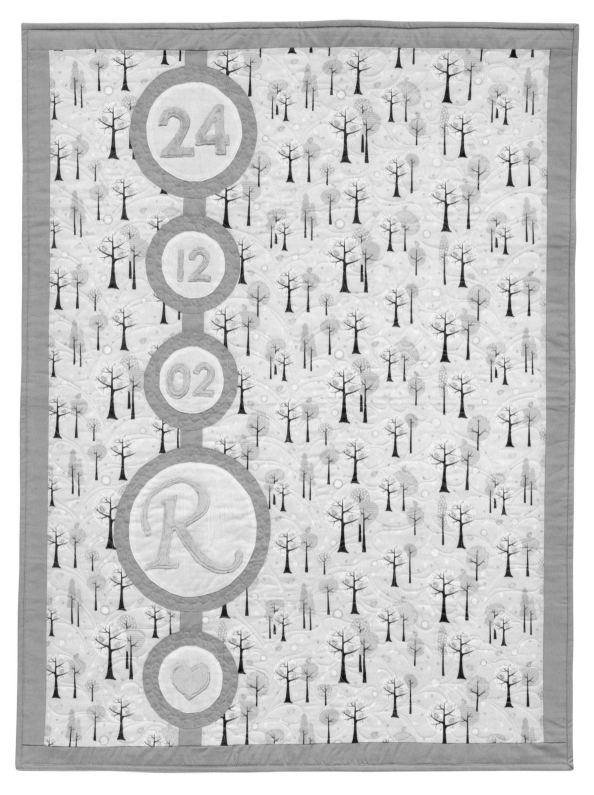

"Peas in a Pod," pieced and appliquéd by Myra Harder; quilted by Katie Friesen

Peas in a Pod

I love this quilt because it's the perfect place to showcase all the information that's unique to your little one. You can fill the circles with dates, names, initials, or fun shapes. Keep all of Baby's important information as close as peas in a pod.

MATERIALS

Yardage is based on 42"-wide cotton fabric and 60"-wide plush fabric.

1⅓ yards of light-pink print cotton for background
1⅛ yards of dark-pink print cotton for border, rings, and binding
⅓ yard of white solid cotton for circles
⅓ yard of green plush fabric for letters, numbers, and heart
1½ yards of fabric for backing
40" x 48" piece of batting
Template plastic

CUTTING

Referring to "Making a Template" on page 37, make a plastic template of the circle patterns for cutting the fabric pieces. The circle patterns are on page 63. The number and heart patterns are on pages 62–64. Refer to "Monograms" on page 11 to make a letter pattern. Refer to "Appliqué the Plush Way" on page 7 and "Appliqué the Needle-Turn Way" on page 8.

From the *lengthwise grain* of the light-pink print, cut:
1 strip, 22" x 42½"
1 strip, 9" x 42½"

From the dark-pink print, cut:
4 strips, 2" x 42"
2 strips, 2" x 35"
5 strips, 2½" x 42"
1 circle, 10" diameter
1 circle, 8" diameter
3 circles, 6" diameter

From the white solid, cut:
1 circle, 8" diameter
1 circle, 6" diameter
3 circles, 4" diameter

From the green plush, cut:
Letter of your choice
Numbers of your choice
1 heart (optional)

ASSEMBLING THE QUILT TOP

1. Sew the dark-pink 2" x 42" strips together end to end. From the pieced strip, cut three 42½"-long strips.

2. Sew dark-pink 42½"-long strips to opposite sides of the light-pink 9"-wide strip. Sew the light-pink 22"-wide strip to the right side of the unit as shown in the quilt assembly diagram below. Then sew the remaining dark-pink 42½"-long strip to the right side of the unit. Press all seam allowances toward the dark-pink strips.

3. Sew dark-pink 2" x 35" strips to the top and bottom of the quilt top. Press the seam allowances toward the dark-pink strips.

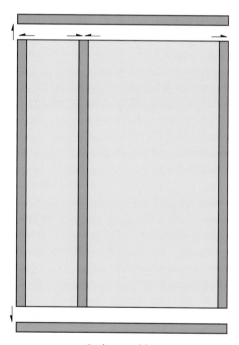

Quilt assembly

ADDING THE APPLIQUÉ

1. Starting at the top, position the dark-pink circles on the dark-pink strip in the following order: 8", 6", 6", 10", and 6", spacing the circles approximately 1" apart. Referring to "Appliqué the Needle-Turn Way" on page 8, appliqué the circles in place.

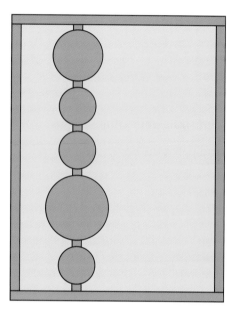

2. Starting at the top, center a white circle atop each dark-pink circle in the following order: 6", 4", 4", 8", and 4". Appliqué the circles in place.

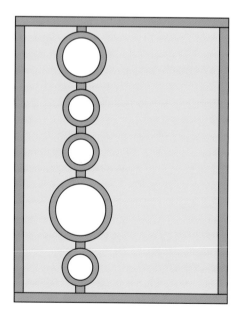

3. Appliqué Baby's birth date, Baby's initial, and a heart in the circles, centering each shape. In Canada, we place the day first, followed by the month, and then the year. If you're in the United States, you might want to put the month first. Refer to the photo on page 58 for placement guidance. The circles are the perfect place to highlight personal information—be creative and add whatever appliqué shapes you'd like.

FINISHING THE QUILT

For detailed instructions on finishing techniques, refer to "Finishing Your Quilt" on page 13.

1. Cut and piece the backing fabric so it's 3" to 6" larger than the quilt top. Layer the quilt top with batting and backing. Baste the layers together.

2. Hand or machine quilt as desired.

3. Square up the quilt sandwich.

4. Use the dark-pink 2½"-wide strips to make and attach the binding.

❖ **Quilting Suggestions**

Choose quilting motifs to reflect whom the quilt is for. The pink, girly quilt features large flowing feathers, and the black-and-white boy's quilt below was quilted with a continuous swirl design.

❖ **Alternate Colorway**

If you have a special little one in your life whose name contains five letters, try this option, using the circles as spaces for spelling out his or her name! You could also adapt the quilt to feature a longer name, by using smaller circles, or a shorter name, by appliquéing stars or hearts in the extra circles.

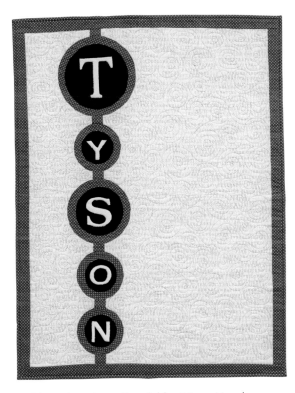

Pieced and appliquéd by Myra Harder; quilted by Katie Friesen

Patterns are reversed for plush appliqué. No seam allowances are needed for plush appliqué. Add seam allowance for hand appliqué.

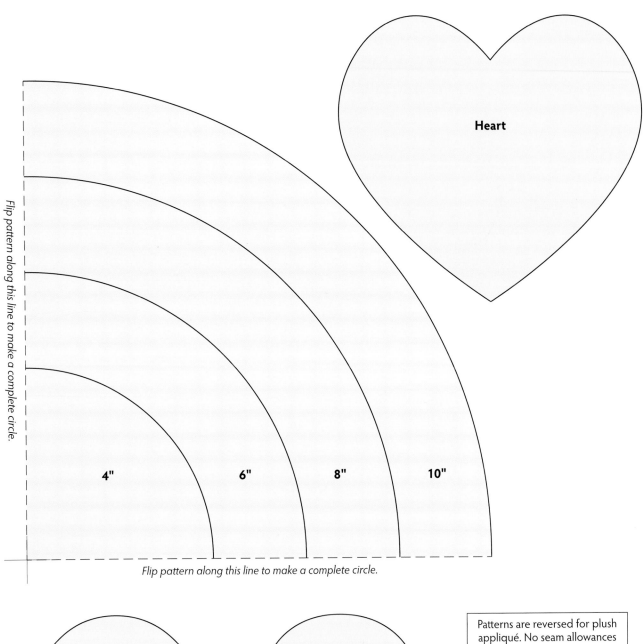

Heart

Flip pattern along this line to make a complete circle.

4" 6" 8" 10"

Flip pattern along this line to make a complete circle.

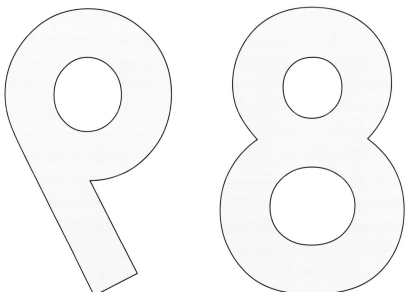

Patterns are reversed for plush appliqué. No seam allowances are needed for plush appliqué. Add seam allowance for hand appliqué.

Numerals for 4" circles

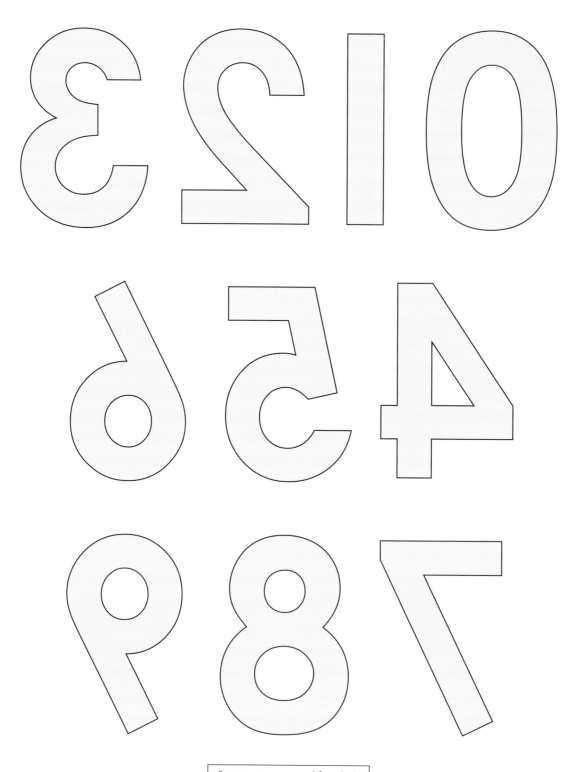

Patterns are reversed for plush
appliqué. No seam allowances
are needed for plush appliqué.
Add seam allowance for
hand appliqué.

Hunter's Star

The colors of fall inspired this very traditional baby quilt. Hunter's Star is a quilt design that's been around for decades, but it still looks fresh and new when paired with warm, lush fabrics. It's a classic quilt that will look wonderful passed down through generations.

MATERIALS

Yardage is based on 42"-wide fabric.

1¼ yards of light print for blocks

⅓ yard *each* of 6 assorted dark prints (light green, medium green, dark green, gold, medium orange, and dark orange) for blocks

½ yard of multicolored print for binding

2⅜ yards of fabric for backing*

41" x 50" piece of batting

Template plastic

*If the backing fabric measures 42" wide after washing and trimming off the selvages, you can use a single width, 1½ yards long.

CUTTING

Referring to "Making a Template" on page 37, make a plastic template of the A and B patterns on page 69 for cutting the fabric pieces.

From *each of 4* assorted dark prints, cut:

2 squares, 7¾" x 7¾"; cut in half diagonally to yield 4 triangles*

3 A pieces

3 A reversed pieces

3 B pieces

*You will only need 3 triangles of each print; 1 will be extra.

From *each* of the 2 remaining assorted dark prints, cut:

2 squares, 7¾" x 7¾"; cut in half diagonally to yield 4 triangles

4 A pieces

4 A reversed pieces

4 B pieces

From the light print, cut:

10 squares, 7¾" x 7¾"; cut in half diagonally to yield 20 triangles

20 A pieces

20 A reversed pieces

20 B pieces

From the multicolored print, cut:

5 strips, 2½" x 42"

"Hunter's Star," pieced by Myra Harder; quilted by Katie Friesen

MAKING THE BLOCKS

For each block, you'll need one dark A piece, one dark A reversed piece, one dark B piece, and one dark triangle that all match. You'll also need two light A pieces, one light A reversed piece, one light B piece, and one light triangle. Instructions are for making one block.

1. Arrange two dark A pieces and one light B piece as shown. Flip one of the dark A pieces over on top of the light B piece, right sides together and aligned as shown. The triangle tip should extend ¼" beyond the B piece. Sew together.

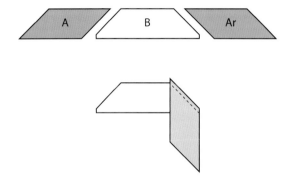

2. Attach the other dark A piece to the opposite end of the unit in the same manner. Press the seam allowances toward the dark A pieces.

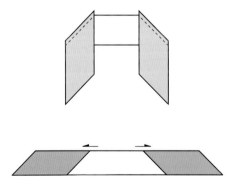

3. Repeat steps 1 and 2 with a light A piece, a light A reversed piece, and a dark B piece. Press the seam allowances toward the dark B piece.

4. Sew a triangle to the short edge of each star-point unit made in steps 1–3, matching the triangle fabric to the center fabric of the star-point units. Don't worry if your edges don't match at this stage; the triangles are slightly oversized and will be trimmed later. For the dark triangle, press the seam allowances toward the triangle; for the light triangle, press the seam allowances toward the star-point units.

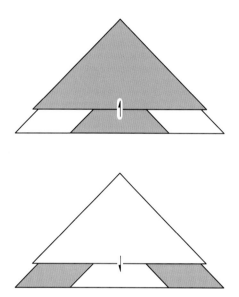

5. Sew the resulting triangle units together to create a block, making sure that the seam intersections of the A and B pieces match. Press the seam allowances toward the star-point unit with the dark center.

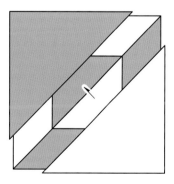

6. Line up the diagonal line on a square ruler with the diagonal seam on the block and align the edge of the ruler with the raw edges of the A pieces. The inner point of opposite star points should be 2½" from the edges of the block. Trim the right and top edges of the block. Rotate the block 180°, align the ruler on the block in the same way, and trim the other two sides of the block to make a 9½" square.

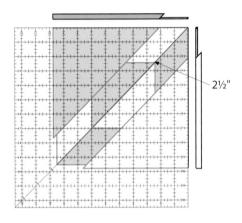

2½"

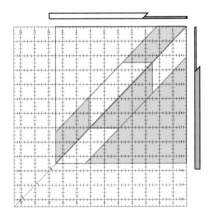

7. Repeat steps 1–6 to make a total of 20 blocks.

ASSEMBLING THE QUILT TOP

1. Lay out the blocks in five rows of four blocks each, rotating the blocks as shown in the quilt assembly diagram below to create stars.

2. Sew the blocks together in rows. Press the seam allowances in opposite directions from row to row. Join the rows and press the seam allowances in one direction.

Quilt assembly

FINISHING THE QUILT

For detailed instructions on finishing techniques, refer to "Finishing Your Quilt" on page 13.

1. Cut and piece the backing fabric so it's 3" to 6" larger than the quilt top. Layer the quilt top with batting and backing. Baste the layers together.

2. Hand or machine quilt as desired.

3. Square up the quilt sandwich.

4. Use the multicolored 2½"-wide strips to make and attach the binding.

✤ Quilting Suggestions

To bring the feel of the outdoors to this quilt, the light areas are quilted with rows of small touching circles, like small pebbles. The quilting makes the print fabrics really stand out and gives a wonderful texture to this classic quilt.

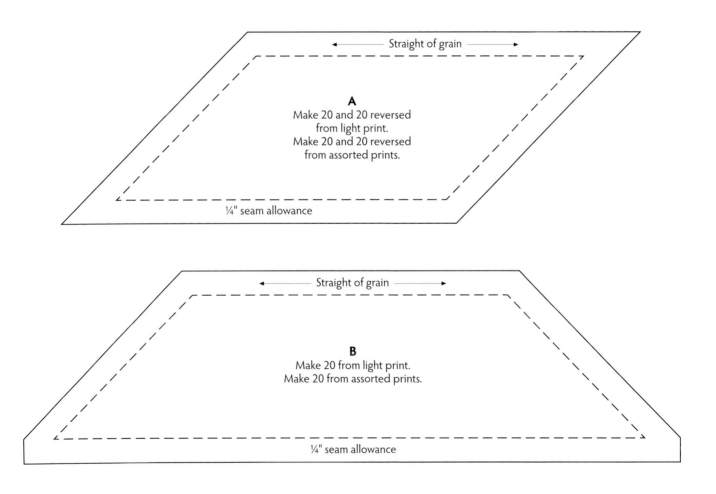

Straight of grain

A
Make 20 and 20 reversed
from light print.
Make 20 and 20 reversed
from assorted prints.

¼" seam allowance

Straight of grain

B
Make 20 from light print.
Make 20 from assorted prints.

¼" seam allowance

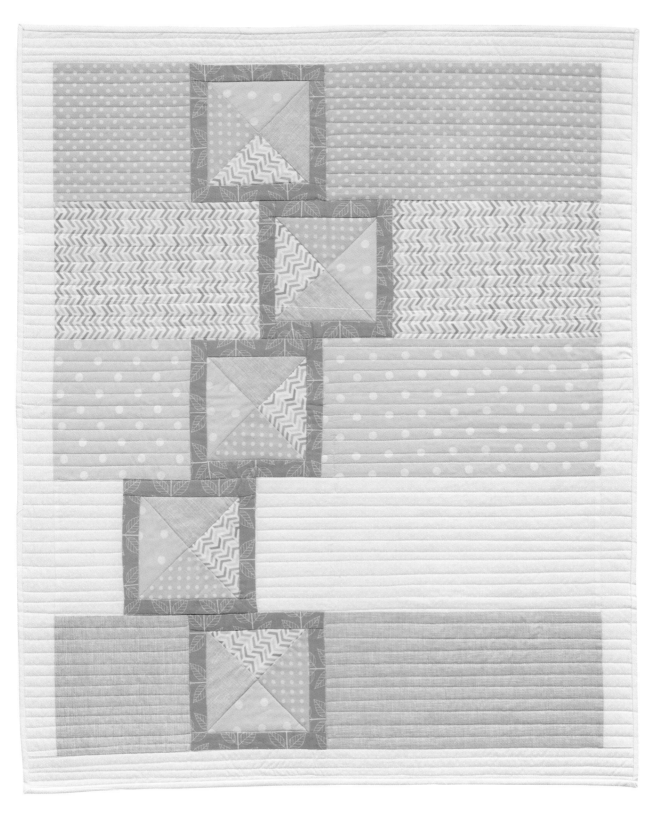

"Jack's Boxes," pieced by Myra Harder; quilted by Katie Friesen

Jack's Boxes

Playing with boxes is something children like to do. They stack the shapes as high as they can, and laugh as their creation falls down. You can have just as much fun making this block quilt—the boxes may look unsteady, but they will never fall.

MATERIALS

Yardage is based on 42"-wide fabric.

⅓ yard *each* of green, white, lavender, and aqua prints for blocks and horizontal rows

1 yard of white solid for horizontal row, border, and binding

¼ yard of teal print for blocks

2⅜ yards of fabric for backing*

41" x 49" piece of batting

*If the backing fabric measures 42" wide after washing and trimming off the selvages, you can use a single width of 1½ yards.

CUTTING

From the white solid, cut:
1 strip, 8½" x 20½"
1 strip, 4½" x 8½"
2 strips, 2½" x 40½"
2 strips, 2½" x 36½"
5 strips, 2½" x 42"

From the green print, cut:
1 strip, 8½" x 16½"
1 square, 8½" x 8½"
3 squares, 5⅛" x 5⅛"; cut in half diagonally to yield 6 triangles (1 is extra)

From the white print, cut:
2 strips, 8½" x 12½"
3 squares, 5⅛" x 5⅛"; cut in half diagonally to yield 6 triangles (1 is extra)

From the lavender print, cut:
1 strip, 8½" x 16½"
1 square, 8½" x 8½"
3 squares, 5⅛" x 5⅛"; cut in half diagonally to yield 6 triangles (1 is extra)

From the aqua print, cut:
1 strip, 8½" x 16½"
1 square, 8½" x 8½"
3 squares, 5⅛" x 5⅛"; cut in half diagonally to yield 6 triangles (1 is extra)

From the teal print, cut:
5 strips, 1½" x 42"; crosscut into:
    10 strips, 1½" x 8½"
    10 strips, 1½" x 6½"

MAKING THE BLOCKS

1. Arrange one green, one lavender, one aqua, and one white print triangle as shown. Join the triangles into pairs along their short edges. Press the seam allowances as indicated. Join the pairs to make a center unit. Press the seam allowances in one direction. Make five units.

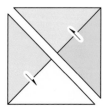 

Make 5.

2. Sew teal 1½" x 6½" strips to opposite sides of a center unit. Press the seam allowances toward the teal strips. Sew teal 1½" x 8½" strips to the top and bottom of the unit to complete the block. Press the seam allowances toward the teal strips. Make a total of five blocks.

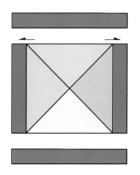 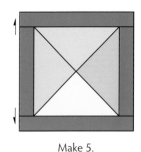

Make 5.

ASSEMBLING THE QUILT TOP

1. Arrange the blocks, squares, and strips in five horizontal rows as shown. Join the pieces into rows. Press the seam allowances away from the blocks. Join the rows and press the seam allowances in the directions indicated.

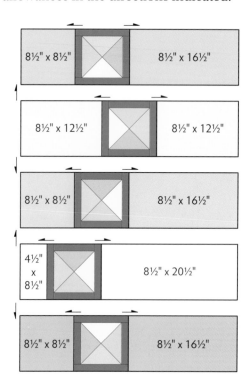

2. Sew the white-solid 40½"-long strips to opposite sides of the quilt top. Press the seam allowances toward the white strips. Sew the white-solid 36½"-long strips to the top and bottom of the quilt top to complete the border. Press the seam allowances toward the white strips.

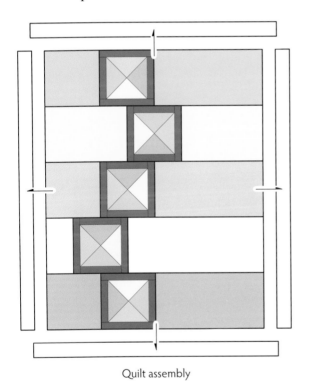

Quilt assembly

FINISHING THE QUILT

For detailed instructions on finishing techniques, refer to "Finishing Your Quilt" on page 13.

1. Cut and piece the backing fabric so it's 3" to 6" larger than the quilt top. Layer the quilt top with batting and backing. Baste the layers together.

2. Hand or machine quilt as desired.

3. Square up the quilt sandwich.

4. Use the white-solid 2½"-wide strips to make and attach the binding.

❖ Quilting Suggestions

There are many fun ways to quilt this project. With "Jack's Boxes," you have a unique opportunity to play. For a very modern feel, quilt horizontal lines, as shown in the quilt photo on page 70. However, this is a great project to try using a different quilting design on each horizontal row. This can be a good place to practice quilting designs that you always wanted to try.

"Gift-Wrapped," pieced and embroidered by Myra Harder; quilted by Katie Friesen

Gift-Wrapped

Babies are so special they should come gift-wrapped. Add Baby's initial to the patchwork box, and then wrap this quilt around that perfect little one.

MATERIALS

Yardage is based on 42"-wide fabric.

¾ yard of red print #1 for embroidered block background and binding

⅝ yard of white print for sashing and border

⅝ yard of red print #2 for upper-right corner

⅜ yard of red print #3 for lower-right corner

⅓ yard of red print #4 for upper-left corner

1 fat quarter (18" x 21") of red print #5 for lower-left corner

1⅜ yards of fabric for backing

39" x 47" piece of batting

White 6-strand embroidery floss for monogram letter

White pencil

CUTTING

From the white print, cut:

2 strips, 3½" x 36½"

2 strips, 3½" x 34½"

2 strips, 2½" x 42"; crosscut into:

    1 piece, 2½" x 20½"

    1 piece, 2½" x 13½"

    1 piece, 2½" x 4½"

    1 piece, 2½" x 3½"

    12 pieces, 1½" x 2½"

4 squares, 1½" x 1½"

From red print #1, cut:

1 square, 10½" x 10½"

16 squares, 1½" x 1½"

5 strips, 2½" x 42"

From red print #2, cut:

1 piece, 18½" x 20½"

1 piece, 5½" x 13½"

From red print #3, cut:

1 piece, 9½" x 13½"

1 piece, 4½" x 5½"

From red print #4, cut:

1 piece, 8½" x 20½"

1 piece, 3½" x 5½"

From red print #5, cut:

1 piece, 3½" x 9½"

1 piece, 4½" x 5½"

ASSEMBLING THE QUILT TOP

1. It's easier to embroider the initial on the red #1 square before assembling the quilt. Referring to "Monograms" on page 11, choose your favorite font and print out a letter to fit the 10½" square. Lightly trace the letter onto the red square using a white pencil. Use two strands of white embroidery floss to embroider the letter, referring to "Embroidery" on page 9 as needed.

2. Join four 1½" red #1 squares and three 1½" x 2½" white pieces to make a pieced strip as shown. Press the seam allowances toward the red squares. Make four strips.

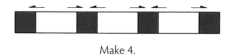

Make 4.

3. Sew pieced strips from step 2 to opposite sides of the embroidered square. Press the seam allowances toward the center.

4. Sew a 1½" white square to each end of the two remaining pieced strips from step 2. Then sew the strips to the top and bottom of the embroidered square. Press the seam allowances toward the center.